PocketMod get started

Table of contents

What's a PocketMod?

Since 2005 the "PocketMod" has been a way to stay organized. Full sized organizers are bulky and are sometimes difficult to keep with you. Nothing is better than a folded up piece of paper. With the PocketMod, you can carry your required notes, keep them organized in any way you want then easily copy your new notes to your computer, tablet, or planner later on.

Directly from the pocketmod.com web site...
"The PocketMod is a small book with guides on each page. These guides or templates (or widgets), combined with a unique folding style, enable a normal piece of letter sized paper to become the ultimate note card. It is hard to describe just how incredibly useful the PocketMod is."

I've always wondered, where did the

name "PocketMod" come from, so I asked Chad Adams, the designer and mastermind behind "PocketMod".

"At the time it came out, there was a lot of talk about "mod-ing" things, like mod-ing your toothbrush, your computer, your life. I wanted a personal organizer that wasn't electronic. Modifying what's in my pocket - PocketMod." - Chad Adams

This book will show you how to make and customize a PocketMod so you can Mod your own pocket. Don't forget, they are cheap to make (one sheet of paper) and they are recyclable.

Widgets

Here we list all the built in pages that are available as of today. On the following few pages you will see each "widget" or page that you can currently build into your PocketMod.

Cover
Blank
writing guides
Lines
Large grid
Medium grid
Small grid
Table
Story board
calendar
Today
Tomorrow
This week
Next week
Weekly (no dates)
Monthly (no dates)
Deadline plotter

Appointment timesheet
This year
Next year
organizers
Simple list
Task list
Shopping list
Contacts 2-people
Task list Lines with check boxes 14 lines
Food diary
personal
Custom Page 1
information (rss)
Weather (asks for zip code)
Time magazine
Wired magazine
Custom (RSS)
Image
Reference
Conversion
Formula (doesn't work)
Tip table low
Tip table high
Morse code table
Dvorák keyboard layout
Games

Dots
Soduku (blank)
Soduku blank
Tic Tac Toe (15 sets)
Miscellaneous
Folding guide (how to fold a PocketMod)
Franklin's virtues (Benjamin)
Emergency cobtact information

Here's what they look like

Cover

- PocketMod -

The PocketMod is a small book with
guides on each page in which you
arrange. These guides or templates,
combined with a unique folding style,
enable a normal piece of paper to
become the ultimate note card!

If lost, return to:

Name:

Address:

City: State: Zip:

Phone:

Email:

copyright © 2007-2008 pocketmod.com

Blank

Writing Guides

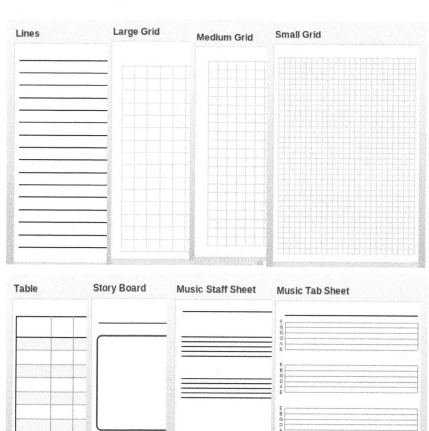

Lines | Large Grid | Medium Grid | Small Grid

Table | Story Board | Music Staff Sheet | Music Tab Sheet

9

Calendar

Today

30 Monday

Tomorrow

1 Tuesday

This Week

30	Monday
1	Tuesday
2	Wednesday
3	Thursday
4	Friday
5	Saturday

Next Week

7	Monday
8	Tuesday
9	Wednesday
10	Thursday
11	Friday
12	Saturday

Weekly

- Monday
- Tuesday
- Wednesday
- Thursday
- Friday
- Saturday
- Sunday

Monthly

Deadline Plotter

Appointm

This Year

2013

Next Year

2014

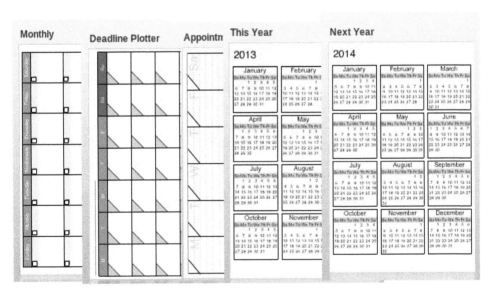

Organizers

...ple List

_____
_____
_____
_____
_____
_____
_____
_____
_____
_____
_____
_____

Task List

_____

- ☐ _____
- ☐ _____
- ☐ _____
- ☐ _____
- ☐ _____
- ☐ _____
- ☐ _____
- ☐ _____
- ☐ _____
- ☐ _____

Shopping List

Shopping List

- ☐
- ☐
- ☐
- ☐
- ☐
- ☐
- ☐
- ☐
- ☐
- ☐
- ☐
- ☐
- ☐
- ☐

...ntacts

Contacts

Check Book

Finance

Date	TRANSACTION	Amount

Total

Food Diary

Food Diary

	Amount	Meal/Snack	Time	Activity
Breakfast				
Lunch				
Dinner				
Snacks/Other				

11

Personal

Custom Page 1

Title

Custom text goes here. It is remembered!

Information

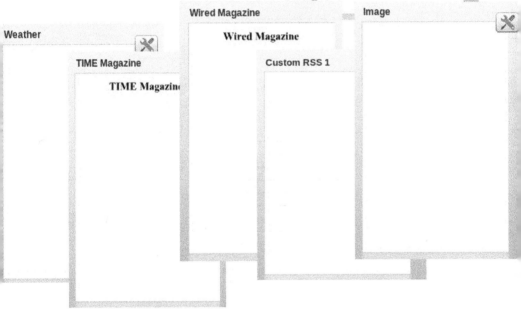

Weather

TIME Magazine

TIME Magazine

Wired Magazine

Wired Magazine

Custom RSS 1

Image

Reference

versions

version Reference

im
= 4 qt = 8 pints = 16 cups = 128 ounces
r = 1.05 quart, 1 quart = 0.946 liter, 1 pint = 473 ml
ibic ft = 7.48 gal, 1 cubic yd = 27 cubic ft

gth
= 1760 yd = 5280 feet = 1.609 km
= 3ft, 1 ft = 12 in, 1 in = 2.54 cm
iter = 1.094 yd = 39.27 in = 100 cm

ɑ
mile = 640 acres, 1 acre = 43560 sq ft
yard = 9 sq ft, 1 sq ft = 144 sq in

s
= 2000 lb = 907 kg, 1 kg = 2.2 lb
nce = 28.35 g, 1 lb = 16 ounces = 453.6 g

sical Constants
er
= 8.33 lb, 1 cubic ft = 62.32 lb
ed of light in a vacuum
.998 x 10^8 m/sec = 186272 miles/sec
ed of sound (20 deg C, 1 atm) in air
m/sec = 769.5 mph = 1129 ft/sec
. Acceleration
.807 m/sec² = 32.17 ft/sec²

ematics
3.14159 26535 89793, e = 2.71828 18284 59045

peratures
9/5(°F - 32), °F = 9/5 °C + 32, °K = °C + 273.2

Formulas

Math Formula Reference

Arithmetic Progression
Sum n terms = (n/2)(2a + (n-1)d), n = 1° term, d = difference

Geometric Progression
Sum n terms = a(1 - r^n)/(1 - r), a = 1° term, r = ratio not 1
Infinite sum when |r| < 1, S = a/(1 - r)

Quadratic Formula
If a x² + b x + c = 0, where a <> 0 then
x = [-b +/- √(b² - 4ac)]/2a

Trigonometry Point (x,y) is in terminal side of A
Sin A = y/r, Csc A = 1/Sin A
Cos A = x/r, Sec A = 1/Cos A
Tan A = y/x, Cot A = 1/Tan A
Sin²A + Cos²A = 1, 1 + Tan²A = Sec²A
r = √(x² + y²), y = r Sin A, x = r Cos A

Geometry
Area circle = π r², circumference = π d = 2π r
Area triangle = (1/2)bh, perimeter = x + h + c
Area rectangle = lw, perimeter = 2l + 2w
Volume of box = l w h, sphere = (4/3) π r³
Surface area of sphere = 4 π r²

Analytic Geometry
Distance formula d = √[(x1 - x2)² + (y1 - y2)²]
Slope = m = (y2 - y1)/(x2 - x1)
Line y = m x + b where m = slope and b = y intercept
Circle centered at (h,k)
r² = (x - h)² + (y - k)²

Tip Table Low

Tip Table					$1 - $50
Amount	15%	20%	Amount	15%	20%
$1.00	$.15	$.20	$26.00	$3.90	$5.20
2.00	.30	.40	27.00	4.05	5.40
3.00	.45	.60	28.00	4.20	5.60
4.00	.60	.80	29.00	4.35	5.80
5.00	.75	1.00	30.00	4.50	6.00
6.00	.90	1.20	31.00	4.65	6.20
7.00	1.05	1.40	32.00	4.80	6.40
8.00	1.20	1.60	33.00	4.95	6.60
9.00	1.35	1.80	34.00	5.10	6.80
10.00	1.50	2.00	35.00	5.25	7.00
11.00	1.65	2.20	36.00	5.40	7.20
12.00	1.80	2.40	37.00	5.55	7.40
13.00	1.95	2.60	38.00	5.70	7.60
14.00	2.10	2.80	39.00	5.85	7.80
15.00	2.25	3.00	40.00	6.00	8.00
16.00	2.40	3.20	41.00	6.15	8.20
17.00	2.55	3.40	42.00	6.30	8.40
18.00	2.70	3.60	43.00	6.45	8.60
19.00	2.85	3.80	44.00	6.60	8.80
20.00	3.00	4.00	45.00	6.75	9.00
21.00	3.15	4.20	46.00	6.90	9.20
22.00	3.30	4.40	47.00	7.05	9.40
23.00	3.45	4.60	48.00	7.20	9.60
24.00	3.60	4.80	49.00	7.35	9.80
25.00	3.75	5.00	50.00	7.50	10.00

Table Hi

Table					$50 - $100
ount	15%	20%	Amount	15%	20%
.00	$7.65	$10.20	$76.00	$11.40	$15.20
.00	7.80	10.40	77.00	11.55	15.40
.00	7.95	10.60	78.00	11.70	15.60
.00	8.10	10.80	79.00	11.85	15.80
.00	8.25	11.00	80.00	12.00	16.00
.00	8.40	11.20	81.00	12.15	16.20
.00	8.55	11.40	82.00	12.30	16.40
.00	8.70	11.60	83.00	12.45	16.60
.00	8.85	11.80	84.00	12.60	16.80
.00	9.00	12.00	85.00	12.75	17.00
.00	9.15	12.20	86.00	12.90	17.20
.00	9.30	12.40	87.00	13.05	17.40
.00	9.45	12.60	88.00	13.20	17.60
.00	9.60	12.80	89.00	13.35	17.80
.00	9.75	13.00	90.00	13.50	18.00
.00	9.90	13.20	91.00	13.65	18.20
.00	10.05	13.40	92.00	13.80	18.40
.00	10.20	13.60	93.00	13.95	18.60
.00	10.35	13.80	94.00	14.10	18.80
.00	10.50	14.00	95.00	14.25	19.00
.00	10.65	14.20	96.00	14.40	19.20
.00	10.80	14.40	97.00	14.55	19.40
.00	10.95	14.60	98.00	14.70	19.60
.00	11.10	14.80	99.00	14.85	19.80
.00	11.25	15.00	100.00	15.00	20.00

Morse Code

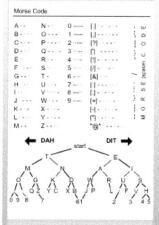

```
A ·-      N -·      0 -----    [.] ·-·-·-
B -···    O ---     1 ·----    [,] --··--
C -·-·    P ·--·    2 ··---    [?] ··--··
D -··     Q --·-    3 ···--    ['] ·----·
E ·       R ·-·     4 ····-    [!] -·-·--
F ··-·    S ···     5 ·····    [/] -··-·
G --·     T -       6 -····    [&] ·-···
H ····    U ··-     7 --···    [:] ---···
I ··      V ···-    8 ---··    [;] -·-·-·
J ·---    W ·--     9 ----·    [=] -···-
K -·-     X -··-              [-] -····-
L ·-··    Y -·--              [_] ··--·-
M --      Z --··             "@" ·--·-·
```

MORSE CODE

Dvorak Keyboard

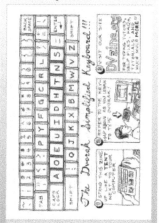

13

Games

Dots

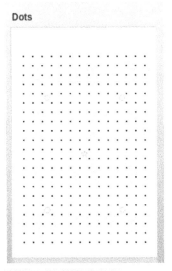

SuDoku

SoDoku

Fill in the grid so that every row, every column, and every 3x3 box contains the digits 1 through 9.

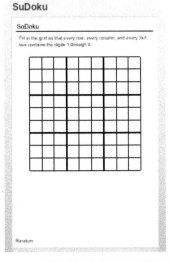

Random

SuDoku Blank

SoDoku

Fill in the grid so that every row, every column, and every 3x3 box contains the digits 1 through 9.

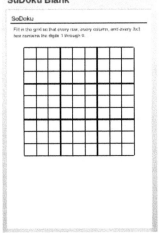

Tic Tac Toe

14

Miscellaneous

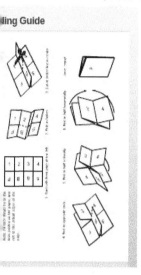

Franklin's Virtues

The 13 virtues of Benjamin Franklin

	S	M	T	W	T	F	S
TEMPERANCE:							
SILENCE:							
ORDER:							
RESOLUTION:							
FRUGALITY:							
INDUSTRY:							
SINCERITY:							
JUSTICE:							
MODERATION:							
CLEANLINESS:							
TRANQUILLITY:							
CHASTITY:							
HUMILITY:							

Emergency

In case of emergency!

Blood Type: _____

Medications:

Special Instructions:

Emergency Contact:

Name

Address

City   State   Zip

Phone

Email

15

Are you like me?

I was the first kid on the block to get a Sharp Wizard 256. I used it a lot. I took it everywhere I went. I bought an IR transfer gizmo that let me back up everything in my Wizard to my PC. Then one day, it stopped working.

When the Palm III arrived. I got one, I loved it. I dropped and broke it, so I got another one. I started using Time & Chaos Software with a program to synchronize everything to my Palm organizer. It all worked perfectly for me. I pressed the appointment button and, bam, there they were. Same with my contacts. It was great! It was fast. A set of charged batteries worked for a couple of weeks. I dropped the last one on concrete, it didn't survive.

Alas, they are no more. Palm got bought by HP which put the whole company to bed, lock, stock and patents.

I bought a smart phone! Well, after a

couple years, I really wished I could buy another Palm PDA. I have no doubt that the Android phones will get better as technology improves. So will iPhones. Both are slow, a charge doesn't last long and input is very slow and cumbersome.

I loved the short cut keys on the Palm devices.

Thank goodness we have PocketMods.

I just wrote tomorrow's appointment into my PocketMod. I will probably put the appointment into my Google Calendar, but not till I get back to real keyboard. The keyboard on my phone is just about useless. It's not just me, I found that anyone who ever used a Palm device for any length time, just can't stand using a current cell phone as a note taking machine.

Let's Make a PocketMod

Open your browser (Google Chrome is best because of the print preview).

Go to the web page www.pocketmod.com

On the right-hand side of the page you will see a link that says "Create a PocketMod", click on this link.

The screen is divided into three parts. The widget part on the left, the working copy of your PocketMod on the right, and the center area where lager samples of the predesigned guides are shown.

Your PocketMod can be remade and changed at any time.

In the widget area, click on the word "Cover". The cover widget will appear in a larger form in the center of the page.

Now click on the Cover page in the center, and hold the left mouse button down and drag the mouse over to the upper most, left most virtual page, actually any blank page of the virtual (make believe) PocketMod will do - on the right side of the screen.

You're done!

Now, let's print your PocketMod. Click on the button that says "Print PocketMod!" (lower right part of the page). If you are using a recent version of the Google Chrome Browser, it will show a fairly accurate representation of the page that you are about to print (or cancel).

After printing or canceling, you can quit the Google Chrome Browser by clicking on File, on the top menu, then click on "Close Window". Bye, bye.

But wait - there's more.

I'll bet you noticed on the "Cover" widget in the upper right-hand corner there is a little icon that looks like a screw driver covered by a wrench. It means the page is customizable.

Most pages (widgets) are not customizable, but there are ones that can be changed, and they might be very valuable to you. There are several customizable pages.

How to make them work?

Easy. Go there (www.pocketmod.com) again. Click on "Create a PocketMod" link, over on the right hand side of the page.

Click on "Cover" again and it will come up in the center again. This time, click on the customize button (in the upper right corner of the cover page in the center) seven input boxes will appear in the center. The input boxes will replace the Cover widget in the center of the screen. The computer wants you to enter your name, address, city, state, zip code, your phone number and email address.

When you're done, click on the [Close] button at the bottom of the center section.

The filled-in cover page should appear. Now you can click and drag the newly finished cover and drop it over the old cover page, or anywhere on your new PocketMod.

When you want to get to any of the hidden widgets, simply click the parent of that page. So you might click on the word "Calendar", or "Organizer" or "Games" to get to those pages under those words,

Paper?

I always used to use plain old white copy paper, but that wasn't necessary, color makes a lot of sense. If I use brightly colored paper for my PocketMod, I never forget it or loose it. When I used to use white paper it tended to blend in with all the other papers on my desk.

Just about any light colored paper will do -- don't forget you must write on the stuff... I have used green apple colored, white (of course), yellow, goldenrod, pale yellow, gray (that wasn't so good), salmon. I'm currently using an off-white color (I think it's called Cream by Hammermill). The good news is any color is cheap, you can buy 500 sheets of your favorite color usually for less than $10. In fact, you can buy a assortment of colors (four or five) at several stores for the same price. Remember, just about any light color will work.

Paper without a texture is best for accepting pen ink. The good news is, that's the cheap stuff. Generally smooth surfaced paper is best at holding ink from your jet printer or toner from your laser printer, better than paper with a texture.

The paper that you use is up to you. The best thing is that with just about any color paper you choose, you can print a year's worth of PocketMod little note books, a new one everyday, for less than ten dollars a year in paper costs.

month, week, day?

About three years ago my job required a new PocketMod each day. I used the "Today" and "Tomorrow" widgets, I made new ones everyday. Each day, I would write my appointments (I called them missions) on the main Today page. There would usually be three missions. Each would get its own page of lines for notes. At each stop, I would write the time of arrival, what was done, what there was yet to do, The time I left. There was usually a document for completed jobs that the customer signed. I kept the used Pocket-Mods for a couple of months, just in case the invoice was wrong or there was a question about the visit. After that, in the recycle bin they would go.

Now, I'm designing software, but I'm at my desk most all the time so a single PocketMod will last me a week. I use the "This Week" widget now and I plan on keeping a year's worth, they will fit in the same box I used to put two months in.

If I have an appointment now, it goes in the day space on the week page. Often the work for the day is written on its own note page (I still have five of those).

Organize your Organizer

As you know by now, the PocketMod is very customizable – and you get to design it! You need to figure out how often you need a new one. How many pages do you need for notes, how many lines will work? Can it be done in eight pages?

For example, this is what I use now: The front cover is really a Simple List that has my name and company name (a lot of my customers don't even know my last name) and phone number. A line with the company address (if I do accidentally leave it behind).

Then two pages of Task list note pages, then a "This week" page. Three more pages of Lines for notes. On the back cover, a "This Year" calendar.

Your PocketMod may very. In fact, it most certainly will. This is mine and works for me, for now. You have already read that I just made a big change from when my PocketMod was very different. Have fun, customize it whenever you want.

Print, Cut, Fold

If you can, use the Google Chrome browser, especially when printing. It should be obvious that the little page graphics on the PocketMod web page (right above the print button) can't be accurate because the pages are shown in portrait mode, in reality, the little pages are printed in Landscape mode. What's good about Google Chrome, is that when you click on the print button, by default, before you print, you will see an accurate picture of how your page will be printed. You may see that how it actually prints might be different than you thought.

On my page printer (Canon MF-3240) a

couple of the widgets show up in the wrong place. Using the Google Chrome Print View (Firefox doesn't have what I'm looking for) you can see how it really will be. Of course, you my not have a problem with your printer. You just have to learn how your printer is going to handle PocketMod pages, so you will know if you need to alter your design so that your page will print out correctly.

As for cutting, this is where the laser printer comes in handy since it always prints the paper completely straight. I simply fold the paper in half lengthwise, then, while the paper is folded, I make the one and only cut with my cheap pair of scissors. I carefully cut along the line between the middle upper two pages and the middle lower two pages. I urge you to watch the cutting / folding video on the PocketMod.com web page lower on the left side. Or look at examples on Youtube. On the next page, you will see the official folding diagram.

Folding Guide

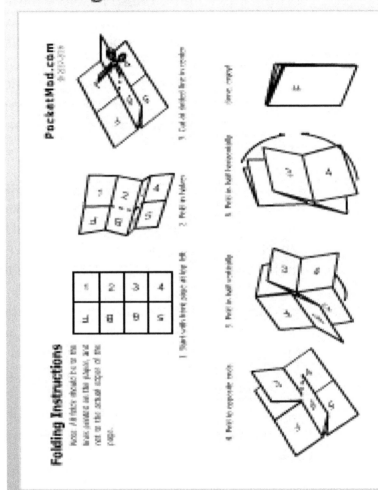

Folding Instructions

Note: All rules should be on the lines printed on this paper, and not at the actual edge of the page.

1. Start with front page at top left.

2. Fold in halves.

3. Cut out dotted line to create...

4. Fold in opposite ends.

5. Fold in half vertically.

6. Fold in half horizontally.

Your copy!

PocketMod.com

Write with pencil / pen

The answer is simple, your favorite writing implement will work just fine. The truth is, you will use your favorite for notes no matter what I suggest.

Read on, I could change your mind.

My affection for mechanical pencils goes back all the way to high school. Back then, if I needed a good pencil, I had to go to the local blueprint shop. Over the years, I have built quite a collection of mechanical pencils. I still frequently use the Pilot Shaker .5mm instrument that I bought in the 80's.

There was a bit of a problem. My customers hated to see me using a pencil on their work tickets - I guess they thought I would erase an item and put something else in.

I had to switch to a pen. In a partner's meeting, I complained about not having a good pen that would fit in my pocket. The next day, one of the partners gave me my first Fisher bullet pen. It was an old beat-up chrome one with black ink (which works fine, BTW).

I'll jump right to the answer here - get a Fisher X-mark bullet pen and use it on your "PocketMod". Here's why, I can't find anything better. When the cap is on it's only 3.6 inches long! It will fit in any pocket. It writes at any angle, even upside down (no matter how hot or cold). Yes, this is the pen that astronauts and cosmonauts take into space. No, I don't have any connection or stock in the Fisher company. I just use the products (you can get them on-line for under $20).

They have been making them the same way for 40 years (they just can't figure out anything better) in the USA!

The cartridges are pressurized with Nitrogen gas and the ball (of the ball point) is made of Tungston-Carbide. The pressurization is what makes them work at the International space station. For us mere mortals here on earth's surface, it just makes them more reliable. They are very popular among police and rescue team workers not to mention members of the military. In fact, just about anyone who works outdoors would benefit from using a Fisher pen.

The Fisher X-mark bullet pen never lets me down. Not only does it work great and last about three times longer than an average pen, but, there are a bunch of colors of ink too. By default you will get medium point black ink cartridge. Some of you may prefer a fine point cartridge. I think there are four different fine point colors. There are nine or ten colors, I believe.

Final Thoughts

Many moons ago, I went to see a prospective client who had no money (it was a non-profit, they *usually* have no unencumbered funds) and they needed to open files in the DOCX format (sent to them by the feds!), I suggested OpenOffice, which could open and edit DOCX files and costs nothing. The office manager didn't like OpenOffice "because there aren't very many books about it on Amazon."

When a friend asked why I wrote a book about a free product, I replied, "There are no books about PocketMod on Amazon". "Oh", was all he said.

OpenOffice worked great for my client. In fact, they have just switched over to the latest version of the office suite. Not only did we land them as a customer, on average, they spent $10 grand with my company every year for the next decade.

I will mention again that I never use the

built in "cover". There is no place to put your company name and it takes up a whole page of the little book. I made my own cover from a Simple List that contains my name, my company name, phone number and address in just two lines leaving most of the page for more notes.

The last thing I have to say is, just between you and me, there might be some plans in the works for upgrades to the PocketMod project. You didn't hear it from me.